Being

A

Magic Mom

Revealing the secrets to being that special magic mom to your kids.

Victoria Odins

Table of contents:

- **<u>Chapter one:</u>**

- **<u>Chapter two:</u>**

Chapter one:

It is only normal for women to ponder whether they are doing a good job as a mom. Constantly we question things like "how to be a good mom?" and "Am I a good mom?"

All mothers deal with the issue of whether she is a good mom and doing a good job as a mother.

It's only reasonable to worry about our children. And anytime one of them does anything wrong, we question ourselves whether we did something to create the behavior. In such moments, we may find ourselves asking, "am I a good mom?"

In periods of doubt, it is easy for us to start over analyzing everything beginning to wonder whether we belong in the good parents club!

So how do you be a good mother? Are there particular attributes I should have? Should I do certain things? Say certain things? Say yes or no to my kids more? How can we define, "What is a good mother?"

What is a Good Mother?

Many of us question, What is a good mother and what traits does she have?

First of all, when we speak about what is a good mother we need to recognize this does not imply perfection! No parent is flawless nor do we want to be ideal, do we?

A good mother tries to be the best she can be. Along her path of parenthood she makes errors, she confesses them, then she dusts herself off and tries again.

That's the beauty of how to be a good parent, she simply continues striving to be the best she can be.

A good mother is unselfish but also knows that she does need "me time" to take care of her family.

Good parents educate their children right from wrong even when it is challenging. They are there for their kids when they need them most, but then let them fly on their own when they are ready.

And when good parents' kids stumble, they are there to pick them up, brush them off, and encourage them to simply keep trying!

There are so many more attributes that makeup what constitutes a good mother. So how can we be good moms? How can we attain the good mom category?

How to Be a Good Mom:

So, of course, there is the age-old issue of how to be a good mom. What do we do to obtain a good mom's status in life?

- Release the inner critic.

Being a good parent implies that you relinquish your inner critic.

No mother should ever compare herself to any other parent. Just like children, no two moms are similar, and each parenting style has its place.

We are always our own harshest critics, and it is all too tempting to compare ourselves to Susie Homemaker or Cathy Corporate, and every other parent we meet on Instagram.

We frequently find ourselves questioning why can't I be more like (put in the blank...) but what we don't recognize at that point is that we are often comparing our worst to their greatest

So when we release our inner critic we do start feeling like we are doing a wonderful job and genuinely belong in the good parents' group.

- Your best is good enough.

We all want to do our best, but trouble arises when we feel that our best isn't good enough.

No matter what we do, we could feel that our efforts fall short, but simply consider for a minute how your son or daughter views things, particularly when they're young.

Do you think kids will notice that mum never had the money to get them the Halloween costume they wanted?

No, instead kids will recall the good times they had helping you create their costumes, even if those outfits never came out precisely properly.
Kids won't remember the stuff that they had, but they will remember the moments that you made together.

- Take better care of yourself so that your best is feasible.

Self-care is a crucial component of becoming a mother. A mom who doesn't take care of herself is unable to take care of her children.

For example, a woman who is severely ill and doesn't take the time to go to the doctor may get weaker and weaker until she can't even get up to fetch her kid food.

On the other hand, if she went to the doctor and received some antibiotics, the sickness wouldn't have been so awful and it would all have been over in a few days.

The same is true of healthy moms.

A mother who never takes time off for herself will feel anxious and unwanted. When she feels worried and unwanted, she is unable to love others, particularly her children.

So take the time for yourself. Read a book, bathe in the tub, exercise, and get a pedicure. Whatever it is that will help you feel better and come back rejuvenated, do it so you can maintain being a wonderful parent.

- Less is more.

Children, particularly when they are young, love the basic pleasures in life.

Kids may not recall the great lengths you went to throw them the ideal birthday party.

They won't recall the enormous pile of gifts.

But kids will remember that one modest wonderful present you purchased or that particular mother and I trip to the ice cream shop.

A child's concentration is distributed onto so many things all at once, yet these tiny moments you create will cast a brilliant light on your child's memory.

- Communication is the key to being a good parent.

Communication is crucial when we are trying to find out how to be a good parents.

Regardless matter how much your kid does or doesn't speak to you, communication is about far more than the number of words that come out of your child's lips.

It's about being actively interested in their hobbies.

Spend some time listening to your son's music or sit and play video games with them.

Just remember that knowing what interests your kid has will provide you an insight into him that you never would be able to have otherwise, even if you attempt to begin a discussion with him.

No matter if you are busy if your kids start talking to you (especially those teenagers) listen. This is when they could need you the very most.

Establish strong communication early with your kids so that when parenting them becomes more challenging you have years of experience interacting with them.

- Date your kids separately.

Every kid wants to feel important, and one of the greatest ways to make your children significant is to spend time with each of them individually.

Sure, family time is crucial, but make sure that you have some time set out for each kid, and utilize this time to connect and learn about their hobbies.

- Set Reasonable Expectations

Setting fair expectations is one of the major secrets of how to be a successful parent.

When you have tiny ones running about you can't expect the home to be pristine. Just as when you have adolescents you can't expect them to tell you everything occurring in their lives down to the finest detail.

As we establish fair expectations women are happy, are less worried and life appears to run smoothly for everyone in the family.

- Do less well.

Often we feel like we have to be Super Mom, wear boots and a cape, and fly about and do everything.

We believe we have to have a flawlessly clean house all the time, assist our kids with their schoolwork, study and make a presentation that wows our customers during the dinner hour, and yet have a hot, homemade meal on the dinner table at home.

Of course, in reality, it's fairly impossible to accomplish all of this at the same time, so simply select one thing you can concentrate on and do it well.

Maybe you're not a very good chef, but you have a talent for research and presentations.

Just concentrate on your job presentation and assist your kids' complete homework later over a late supper from the local takeaway.

- Make sure the discipline reflects the offense.

Kids are destined to require discipline in their life. Good mothers analyze each scenario and administer a penalty depending on the offense.

If youngsters are old enough let them assist estimate suitable penalties.

If the child is too little to grasp this, make sure that the penalty is directly tied to what she did.

- Allow your kids to fail.

No parent should ever follow around behind their kid repairing all of their blunders. Of course, it's crucial to be there if your kid makes a significant mistake and to make sure he understands that he can come to you.

But sometimes it is vital to let him fail.

If his girlfriend breaks up with him because he spent too much time playing video games and not enough time with her, let him find out on his own what he did wrong.

It's OK to clue him up, but don't fix it for him.

He will never learn how to live life and repair issues alone if mom is constantly there to make changes.

Remember, being a good enough parent isn't a question of perception. It's a reality that you are already excellent enough. You simply have to think that you are.

- Show physical love.

OK, you knew this one was coming. Physical affection doesn't come easy for everyone, so don't allow your discomfort prevent you from making your kid feel loved. Sit down and let your toddler crawl into your lap. Make hug time pleasant. Scratch your adolescent son's back. Kiss your daughter on the cheek as you snuggle her into bed. There will come a moment when your kids won't be physically there in your life every day, so get the love in now while you can.

- Be truly present.

We know what we need to do to make this happen, but it’s not simple. We need to put down our phones, shut the computers, and stop filling our dishwashers when our children require our attention. Engage in discussions to discover more about them. Put your phone down and listen to what your youngster has to say.

- Be nice.

There is no question we love our children, but love without compassion doesn’t seem particularly loving.

There is no question we love our children, but love without compassion doesn't seem particularly loving.

- Laugh with them.

A successful parent-child connection requires a decent dose of levity. Laugh with your children at what they believe is humorous.

- Discipline calmly.

For many moms, this is the toughest of the seven. Disciplining our children is best done when we aren't heated up or agitated. While yelling at them can feel nice and look to be beneficial, it's actually not. Keeping our calm as we mold our children allows us to discipline with firmness instead of cruelty.

- Use loving words.

A mother's words are strong! Pausing for a minute before we speak to pick our words carefully may be the difference between harsh or flippant remarks and words that build our children up. Do your best to make sure that most of what you say to your children conveys your love and acceptance. Compliment them every day and be careful to avoid these 15 things you should never say to your children.

- Pray with them.

When we pray with our children, we are teaching them that we depend on God. This teaches kids that they can depend on God, too, and that God's love for us is the source of our love for them.

Chapter two:

Becoming a parent may be a little daunting, particularly when advice comes in from all sides. So we've created this handy collection of fast suggestions from in-the-know parents and professionals to help you get started, and give you the confidence you need to embrace your new position. The Best Expert Parenting Advice:

Tips for Mom

Be present

Don't worry too much about eating

Keep an early bedtime

Learn to say "no"

Create tiny customs

Be prepared for ill kids

Parent the kid you have

Have people you can chat toBe a role model

Share responsibility with your partner

Talk to your youngster about money

ReadTake change slowly

Help your infant learn to fall asleep on their own

Establish chores

Trust yourself

Foster independence

Apologize

Take breaks

Encourage sibling harmony

Take safety measures

Tell your youngster tales about yourself

Put down distractions

Go outside

Be silly

Prioritize being a parent, not a friend

Use math

Be consistentDance

Be patient with the "why's"

Teach mannersEncourage thankfulness

Tell them how much you adore them

Live in the moment

You now have permission to stop thinking about your checklist—doing the laundry, pumping, purchasing diapers—and learn to be present with your kid. Enjoy your valuable times together. — Wayne Fleisig, Ph.D.

Chill out about toddler meals

Expect unusual dietary habits. Offer a variety. Don't push, don't panic. They'll eat when they're hungry. — Connie Diekman, R.D., Washington University in St. Louis

Stick to an early bedtime

Your youngster will receive the sleep he needs, and you'll get to replenish your batteries.

—Jodi Mindell, Ph.D., author of Sleeping Through the Night

Say "no"

The better you grow at rejecting down requests that aren't in your child's best interest, the less times you'll need to do so. You can say no once at the store when your youngster begs to purchase a carton of ice cream, or you can say it every night after the carton is sitting in your freezer at home. —David Ludwig, M.D., Ph.D., author of Ending the Food Fight.

Create mini-traditions

Hang balloons around the kitchen table the night before your child's birthday so she wakes up to a memorable day.

Make a humorous noise when it's only you and your kids in an elevator.
Create a handshake that only they know—and preserve it for important events.
—Harley A.
Rotbart, M.D., author of No Regrets Parenting

How to Celebrate Birthdays Without a Big Party

Be ready for ill days

Stock up on rehydration liquids like Pedialyte, Gatorade, or Vitamin Water so you don't have to dash to the store in the middle of the night when your young one is vomiting.
—Wendy Hunter, M.D., Rady Children's Hospital, University of California, San Diego

Know your child
Each kid has a unique blend of talents and difficulties.

Try to personalize your answer to meet the youngster in front of you.
—Eileen Kennedy-Moore, Ph.D., author of Smart Parenting for Smart Kids

Find your crew

Identify the folks you can contact when you need to vent—friends who'll provide their opinion when you ask for it and keep their mouth shut when you don't, and who would drop everything to be there for you and your family (and vice versa) (and vice versa).
Love them fiercely and thank them frequently.
—Lacey Dunkin, single mom of six

Remember, you're a role model
Make being a mom appear desirable to your kid so she'll want to have children and you can be a grandma one day.
If you're usually upset, pouty, or grumbling, she won't be encouraged to become a parent herself.

—Wendy Mogel, Ph.D., author of The Blessing of a Skinned Knee

Let your spouse take control

He's all in, so encourage him to be in charge of bathing, reading, or tummy time (or all three) (or all three).
They're terrific bonding activities—and a chance for you to take a break.
—David L.
Hill, M.D., author of Dad to Dad: Parenting Like a Pro.
Talk about money choices

When you choose a brand of cheese because it's less costly (and just as delicious) or elects to pass on a handbag you like "until it's on sale," explain your logic to your youngster.
—Farnoosh Torabi, mom of two and presenter of the So Money podcast

Read to your kid every single day

It helps cultivate creativity and is time well spent.
—Christine Hohlbaum, mom of two and author of The Power of Slow

Go small with large changes

Bottle to a sippy cup?
Crib to bed?
Of course, you want these adjustments to go well and fast, but that might be overwhelming to your small one.
Let him play with the new cup, or sit and read together in the new bed first.
Once he's adjusted to the new sensory experiences, you may make the transition official.
—Harold S.
Koplewicz, M.D., president of the Child Mind Institute

Help your infant fall asleep on their own

Feed her at the start of your nightly ritual.
After a bath, stories, and snuggling, put her down when she's tired but still awake.
If you feed or rock her to sleep, she'll constantly require your support to drift asleep.
—Dr. Mindell

Establish chores

Have your kids chip in at home by emptying trash cans, making their beds, setting the table, and putting toys away.
Helping out with domestic duties develops self-esteem since you trust them to complete the job.
—Martin R.
Eichelberger, M.D., Safe Kids Worldwide, Children's National Medical Center

Trust your intuition

Even if you can't pinpoint what's wrong when your kid doesn't feel well, your instinct will tell you that he needs to be looked out for.
—Ari Brown, M.D., author of Baby 411

Don't become the butler

Your children are hardwired for competence.
Get children in the habit of hanging their jackets in the closet and putting their filthy items in the hamper at an early age, so you don't have to.
—Dr. Mogel

When you're incorrect, admit it

If you goof up with your child (or your partner), apologize.
This will teach your kids that it's okay to make a mistake as long as you acknowledge it and say you're sorry.

—Alice Domar, Ph.D., author of Finding Calm for the Expectant Mom

Give yourself time-outs

When you're feeling angry, you're less likely to respond to your child helpfully.
You don't have to react instantly.
Taking a brief break helps you settle down and think things through.
—Dr. Kennedy-Moore

Nudge sibling harmony

At dinner, have each child take turns saying what he enjoyed about his brother or sister that day.
This helps kids look for the positives in their siblings rather than the negatives.
—Lacey Dunkin

Open windows from the top

Eliminate the chance of your youngster falling by keeping them closed and fastened on the bottom.
And don't entice her to climb by putting low furniture beneath.
—Dr. Hunter

Like a Boy Scout, be prepared

Never leave the home without at least one change of clothing for each little kid.
—Dr. Hill

Beware of the humblebrag parent

When friends brag about their clever or super talented kid, relax.
Chances are they're exaggerating or lying.
—Dr. Mogel

Tell "age tales"

At night, have your youngster select a number less than your present age.
Then tell her about anything noteworthy that occurred to you at that age.
—Dale McGowan, dad of three and author of Raising Freethinkers

Put down your phone

When you're with your kids, that call/text/e-mail can wait.
They know when you're not paying attention.
—
David Fassler, M.D., author of Help Me, I'm Sad: Recognizing, Treating, and Preventing Childhood and Adolescent Depression

Be without a ceiling

Try to go outdoors together for at least a few minutes every single day and move beneath the sky.
It's an opportunity to abandon screens and sedentary pursuits and develop a rain-or-shine tradition that will benefit your kid for life.
—Wendy
Sue Swanson, M.D., author of Mama Doc Medicine: Finding Calm and Confidence in Parenting

Act silly

Life may be overly serious.
Let your kids watch you laugh, make silly faces, and chase them around the house shouting, "I'm going get you!"
—Dr. Domar

Walk instead of driving

Use your legs for short errands and local playdates.

As you stroll with your youngster, converse, play "I spy," or jump over gaps in the pavement together.
—Dr. Rotbart

Be a parent, not a buddy

Your job isn't to be popular.
Your kids may not always like you at the moment.
But deep down they'll always love you for setting clear expectations.
—Dr. Eichelberger

Make math more fun

Take every opportunity to play with numbers, sizes, and shapes.
Count the oranges and apples as you put them into the bag at the grocery store.
Ask your child which cereal box is the tallest.
Point out the circle in the clock and the rectangle in the window.

—Deborah Stipek, Ph.D., author of Motivated Minds: Raising Children to Love Learning.

Stay consistent with your rules

But first, make sure they're fair.
—Dr. Domar

When you're talked out and tired out from endless demands, turn on some music and just shake off the day.
It's hard not to smile when you're letting loose (and watching your kids dance) (and watching your kids dance).
—Lacey Dunkin

Answer the incessant "why" queries

This is easier said than done, yet young kids are interested in everything in their surroundings.

If you cease responding to their inquiries, kids may stop asking.

—Raquel D'Apice, creator of The Ugly Volvo blog

You don't want to lose priceless digital memories.

Invest in a backup hard drive or a cloud service.

—Darshak Sanghavi, M.D., author of A Map of the Child

Show your youngster how to welcome others

Teach your youngster to establish eye contact, smile, and meet someone new in diverse contexts.

Then have her try it out.
You only have one opportunity to create a first impression.
— Faye de Muyshondt, mom of two and 32 creators of Socialsklz :-) for Success

Let your kid know—through your actions and your words—how much you adore him and what you think is wonderful about him.
—Dr. Fleisig

www.ingramcontent.com/pod-product-compliance
Lightning Source LLC
LaVergne TN
LVHW020534160826
845677LV00015B/4045

* 9 7 9 8 3 5 6 0 8 8 0 0 1 *